GOD'S CREATURES
ON THE FARM

GOD'S CREATURES

ON THE FARM
Our Food and Clothing

by
Debra K. Stuckey

illustrated by
Jules Edler

CONCORDIA®

Publishing House
St. Louis

Copyright © 1986 Concordia Publishing House
3558 S. Jefferson Avenue, St. Louis, MO 63118-3968
Manufactured in the United States of America

Library of Congress Cataloging-in-Publication Data

Stuckey, Debra K., 1959-
  God's creatures on the farm.

  Summary: Describes how God cares for our needs by making farm animals to provide us with warm clothing and nutritious food.

  1. Domestic animals—Religious aspects—Christianity—Juvenile literature. 2. Creation—Juvenile literature. [1. Domestic animals—Religious aspects] I. Edler, Jules, ill. II. Title.
BT746.S79   1986   233'.11   85-17421
ISBN 0-570-04136-8

1   2   3   4   5   6   7   8   9   10   PP   95   94   93   92   91   90   89   88   87   86

**To
Rachel and Joshua**

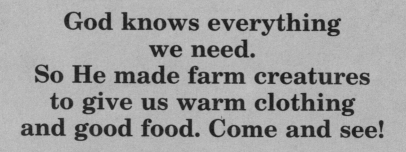

God knows everything
we need.
So He made farm creatures
to give us warm clothing
and good food. Come and see!

The rooster wakes me early
each morning.
"Cock-a-doodle-do!"
he calls.
"See the fine day
God is making for you."

"Moo," says the big,
brown cow.
Her rich, sweet milk
helps me to grow.
God, You knew I'd need that.

"Baa, baa," cry the frisky,
young lambs.
Feel their soft, fluffy wool.
God made it.
Now we can have
warm sweaters.

"Buzz, buzz,"
sing the busy bees.
God sends warm sunshine
so flowers will grow
and the bees can make honey.
M-m-m-m!

"Honk, honk," call the
geese on the pond.
God gives them soft feathers
so we can
make fluffy pillows
or warm coats. How cozy!

The hens in the hen house say,
"Cluck, cluck."
Their fresh eggs
make a tasty breakfast.
God, You sure are good to us!

"Meow," cries a furry,
little kitten.
God even has a job for her.
She chases the mice away
from God's good grain.

"Neigh," calls the horse
in the pasture.
God gives him strong legs
so that he can
run like the wind.
What a fun ride!

Our kind God cares
for our needs.
He made each farm creature
to help us.
God, You sure love us a lot.

Thank You, God!

THE END